MORTAL

MORTAL

POEMS
2007–2016

Thomas Dillon Redshaw

BRIGHTHORSE BOOKS
2017

Brighthorse Books
13202 N. River Drive
Omaha, NE 68112

ISBN: 978-1-944467-04-3

Cover Art: Kit Cornell
Author Photo: Sean O'Brien

For permission to reproduce selections from this book
and for more information about Brighthorse Books
and the Brighthorse Prize, visit us on the web at
brighthorsebooks.com.

i ndílcuimhne ar

Jeannie Rogers

18 May 1948–29 April 2016

CONTENTS

III. FATHER

ᴊᴦ

PIKE

Where an omnibus idles in lucent July, Japanese couples
Come from the nuns' tearoom past postcard racks & snap,
Redundantly, themselves before a blue boat beached in the rushes.

There are two sights of Kylemore Abbey—the Gothick chapel
& this lakeside pastoral, but no Polaroid can develop
The long bronzy thresh of the pike sawing the line
At an oaken oarlock &
                                            plunging deep from the light.
The instinctual hunter betrays the serene Latin
Of these Irish Dames of Ypres, Benedictines all—
A crucifix in each varnished room of the robber baron's castle.

But the sign foresight makes is not the chalk or charcoal
Fish of the catacombs, but the real ravener—slick, toothy,
Y-boned, haunting the glacial chill of Pollacappul—
Implacable, ancient, myopic, deaf to human prayer.

I. VETERAN

DIGGING A RAISED BED

es war wie gras
—BRAHMS

Slicing the ruined grass last August, turning
The dry sod roots up, shaking soil from the fork . . .

I was improvising, not measuring, just laying out
The form by eye and ear, leveling by guesswork
Where the rot-proof timbers would lie,
                       notched
Together at the corners, notched across in the midst,
Four high, spiked down by the five-pound hammer.
Each, each blow a heartbeat forefelt at the news.

Standing up for ease in what once was a chain-linked
Laundry yard in the Fifties, shaded by a silver maple
Blown down near the end of that century &

Staring down at the dirt heaped between the timbers
I find the plastic figurine of a Green Beret or G.I. Joe.

THE DAKOTA

a scene after Jan Steen

An infant dozes through the christening party
Where mother, father, family play the roles
Of domestic pleasures. Parrot-red wine
Falls like a melody into the goblet above
The sleeping child's head. Red & green
Grapes, a skinned orange, shucked oysters
On pewter, clay pipe & musette decorate
The earnest moral
                        that turns inside out
At your corner of the dark bar—sipping, inhaling,
Swallowing, sipping again . . . listening until late
Almost every night to a blue chord, clarinet
Riff or holler . . . hearing lately what we imagine
When we hear *Ave verum corpus.* . . .

DUTCH BLUES

for the weepers
—LOU RAWLS

Long past flicking pan fish out of the river.
Long beyond midnight. Crumpled napkin-wise
Paper towels litter the dinette table.
Glasses smeared with sweet whiskey & beer
Stand sentinel over crumbs of panfried
Crappie, bluegill & pumpkinseed. Queasily,
The cards span out down the river, turning into
That dark bay.
                  We complain blearily together.
"This boy ain't had a decent shit in years." The
Words hang hilarious in the haze.
                                                Listen, again.
"I got caught," factually, as if knowing better
Could not save you. Going Dutch, again.

THE GRAY TREE

after Piet Mondrian

Fog falls on farmland from the Michigan shore
On inland where plats of fallow field square up
To ranks of stick-built, then wafer-boarded,
Then vinyl-sided twin homes—some unbegun,
Others unfinished, others newly empty—garages
Agape.
      Just beyond, overgrown woods appear
When the mist sifts through dripping branches.
Not woods, but a relict orchard.
                    Thick trunks
Paced apart for picking. Water sprouts leap up
& curl from older limbs. Should leaf, then blossom
Ever come again, the fruit will swell & sweeten
Too high for a pointed ladder to reach.

TURKEY BUZZARDS AT BORDE DU LAC

September sunrise and a stiff breeze from the south
& my back to the light that gilds the stand of pine
Behind the mobile home dressed up in brown shingle.

In skies past eagles had come over us there, wheeling
Down out of the blue, white-headed & dark-winged
Conning the sandy foreshore just once before arching
Away to the gray chop of Kabekonah Bay—the pair of them
Bringing a lift of luck that didn't last.

                      So I know
These wings soaring gold just above the pines are
Hatchlings of the season, just fledged, lined up ready
In the updraft to claim what lift morning could provide.

Bending over the scarred green cowl of the Evinrude,
You look up to where I want to point, squint &
Point out that they are too many to be eaglets.

A MISQUOTATION

ruft uns die stimme
—BACH

Talk to him while you work. He will answer,
Michael had said. Bright, warm, dry after a week's worth
Of needful rain. This work is a simple pleasure,

Cutting English thyme, laying out its flavor
Earth to earth end, laying down spray by spray
Of green leaf. Some say it is the hardiest variety.

Fractals, dendrites, growth gives slow
Advantage to one leaf, then another & helps roots
Hoard their woody sugar until cold come.

It is for yourself that you weep.

      At first,
That was right, but not at last, I hope as I stand,
Secateurs in hand, staring south into that
Sudden blue breaking through at the horizon.

WEDNESDAY

like the dew of Hermon
—BERNSTEIN

Still sitting up. Facing south into afternoon.
Breathing on your own at last. Not resting
But striving.

       Hardly is there effort extra
To share a word, yet the green and gold lines
Jump steadily in the face of the monitor. We look
Then into your open face, masked for oxygen,
Into your open eyes, unmasked.

               We cannot
Explain it when the black of your pupils
Grows, and you stare out over the cluttered sill
Straight over city & river, away into the open
Blue above Holman Field

           and after a breath
return to us who listen and look on, who caress
your dear head or press your bruised hand
for you to let us know we are here still.

CREEPING CHARLIE

wer heilet die Schmerzen
—BRAHMS

Listen to what he said. Remember. Listen.
Hard to do—two years later, in a bright June,
The peonies pillowing open magenta & pink
by my brick path, creeping Charlie blooming
up again, in the grass.

      Listen. Remember.
March, so many months ago, casually,
Before your afternoon seminar, turning
Away, out my office door & down
The hall in your ratty, tall raincoat. "I got
Caught."

    The peony has a gold heat
And Swedish ivy a sweet & minty allure
When cut, but rue leaves no wonted scent.

A RED HAT

A Memoir

Seated one Thanksgiving between Elizabeth
& Marie on the divan, like a Red Hat Lady
Perched on a bench at The Lex, you unpinned
That red Spanish hat as if it were no more than
A prop from *Bolero*, or a cap for some consistory,
Saying, "Poor baby, you like it, have it!" or
From the back of the room, insisting, "Really,
Try it on, I believe it fits you just as you are."

II. NINETEEN FORTY-FOUR

ULLARD STEPS

One brown, one white, two mares
stand off as I walk their churned ground
up the hill toward the stile

Three stone steps up, then over,
I put a foot wrong & go down
like a bag of coal, shoulder first,
then face down,

                silent in the moss
at the edge of the road, the breath
gone out of me.

                Deep in that space
waters slip that fill a stone well below
& hoof prints in their circuit
where the ground is soft.

FREEWAY POPPIES

On the road from Greensboro to Old Salem,
coming up on the Kernersville exit, a streak
of tousled vermilion measures away a moment
passed behind the airport van's safety glass.
To walk that stretch would take slow minutes
in that May afternoon.
                              To make a path away
from the highway's curls up to the berm. To walk
slower still amid those silver-green leaves &
nodding, black-centered blooms. To walk so slow,
almost to lie prone and past. To seem gone
& dead to those speeding away in their own lives.

Sown wild along the long shoulder, a bank
of poppies flares red in the five o'clock sun.

AN ISOTOPE

wheat that springeth green
    —AN EASTER CAROL

Kindly, they help you lie dead still
in your clothes, left arm above the head
in the antique posture of grief.
                            I recalled
this room as underground, brick-walled,
but truth took it two storeys up, where I wait
as the tincture of thallium chloride and its
half-life answers the beating heart's hunger
for potassium.
                    Soon the heart weakly glows
sacred as in any pious lithograph, radiating a
wounded shape onto the slowly orbiting
film of measured fact. Loss is a dear salt like
any other, but its half-life remains unknown.

Muted, blows of a pile-driver reach up
from the diggings for the new North Wing.

EMPTY BEACH

The yellow bus had stopped on the north shoulder
of the coast road where it curved inland & west.
black block letters under empty windows
bear the forgotten Puritan names of suburban
Townships. From that door the driver had left
folded open,
            I could see the path across, then
down the berm, under the feathery leafage
of the sumac wood, to the heaped stones, then
shelly sand of the wide & empty beach stretching
flat away, then darkening in neap tide, glistening
just at a far-off blue horizon.
                        That one sight
was why I had been brought in my sleep here
and left to stand bare-headed like someone's child.

1950

Under the clean August heat a child naps
in a dim room on whose yellow wallpaper
float white China temples consecrated
to stylized mercy.
               Waxy, stiff, the paper
shades let in the light of the East, waning
that afternoon. This side of the house rests
now in near shade. Someone has raised
both sashes from their sills so the shades
waver in freshening salt draughts. Tap,
tap of green crocheted pulls,
each a threaded circle.
               Resting light, turn,
turn to glimpse between sill and sash
the latitude of arresting blue—that
unparalleled dream of clear sailing.

GROUND TRUTH

Days of it. Nights of it. The Weather Channel
animating in smears and commas of florid color
streams of digital echo, Doppler signatures
of debris and states in disarray all endlessly
explained in running duets of expertise
sounded and shown above the thin line

typing out names of good Christian towns
that lie splintered and prone aside flooded
highways.
                Poor Tom takes us by the hand
to the brow of our hill. The pickup speared,
the limb crack'd, our dog crushed, and our bedding
shredded across raked fields.

A CUP BY KIT CORNELL

I did not buy the real thing at the market
on Hospital Hill that last summer morning, but
took away the perfect postcard of it—
a bookmark, a memento—as if the glaze
gave a scene we will travel into but not
return from
         —a gray & sandy foreshore,
darker where the tide laps back—
                  and where
we will remain gazing at the blue gleam
lightly turning across darker waters to
the lip of the cup lit up like a line
of low clouds lying easterly on a horizon.

Out there, the cup waits empty & ever
ready to fill, raise, and pass hand-to-hand.

SONG OF THE EARTH

Reading slowly on the open porch
in the early air of an August morning,
I hear the steady strike of a pile driver
off in the parking lot of my old bank
at Selby and Snelling
                                    where Goods
and Mammon raise new properties &
sink underground parking.
                                        The zephyr
carrying that ring wanders, then back
over the Green Line, over the switching yards
offering more clearly than steeples
of nearby chapels on Como or Carter
a pure note rung on the bell of earth.

LOCUST LEAVES

Locust leaves lying in the sun, drying,
drying where a wind left them.
Rising in calm light, the scent
of warmed paper,
                of an unvarnished
windowsill in an attic full of boxes,
banker's boxes of old files, logs of rugs
rolled to save their oriental colors.

This is the path of a summer's exhalation.
A whisp breathed in before the sigh
that curls along and winds their yellow
up. . . .

BEFORE THE WAR

Before the war
Through groves of yew
We walked
Through heavy light.

Before the war
In windowed homes
We spoke
In painted masks.

Before the war
On tables laid in linen
We fed
On silent flesh.

Before the war
Under clouded skies
We slept
Under leaden blankets.

III. FATHER

FLOATERS

In the yellow flash of a blink
Hermes stands, just off to the right
of the Eye & free of the instant flare of
dark capillaries.
                  He is quick.
His beckoning slight,
                         erased
by daylight, by lamplight that floods
the page of sight with a detail there
that draws
            & draws again the focus
of breath. What catches the breath
upon a closer look looks like
a sentence written round the clear
orbit of the pupil & again round
the unfurled color of the iris.

NAP

The implicated eddies of detail
& tide of perspective lapping—
it is a dream I am submerged in.

On the club veranda my father,
Sitting in a blue windbreaker, leaning away
in a deck chair next to me,
      his younger
profile turning just away, his sailing self
looking off.
    Suddenly I weep, weep
& throw my arms around him.

In that sunset harbor, rigging rings
on metal masts & I wake to house wrens
chittering outside my window.

MY FATHER'S FEET

He props himself up at the edge of his painted bed,
arms angled out, hand holding the mattress's edge.
I have lotion and a towel on the floor beside me.
He has a lot to say about the strain of bending
unsteadily to clip his nails, care for his feet
on his own.
                    Kneeling in front of him,
I rub the lotion between my palms and take
one white foot at a time, ankle to toes, easing
the tendons, then palm each heel, each narrow sole
again and again, letting him catch the lotion's scent
of rosemary.
                    On the bed's grained headboard
in faded gold and black someone once stenciled
a dim theorem of a cornucopia spilling out
apples, melons, grapes. This is the least I can do.

FIXING A FENCE

Built of green wood rough sawn
for a rustic look. Set up between
a deck, a garden around an urn,
an overshadowed plot, and woods,
a near marsh, the deer path.

       Painted white
& painted again, peeling off rot
filled with rock putty or plastic wood,
a panel gone, taken apart, then put right
as if his life depended on it, done
& undone, fitted then unfitted

         leaving
a gap to keep him busy, safe,
& keep out what must come
at the leafy end of exhaustion.

OUR FATHER

No longer could he curve the letters
of his name on a used envelope or
fill out the right line of a check. He asked her.

He had found her child's Bible
in the bookrack that ended in owls.
Standing in her bedroom that night
he held it out to her. Would she
write it out for him, that famous
petition? Those words that everyone
knows?
         She wrote it out from memory
on a steno pad she kept in the kitchen.
He kept it folded in a drawer next to his bed
—in a drawer he never opened.

A FALL

Light in the hall. He had fallen,
bathrobe open on waxy flesh, bruises.
Cleaning himself with dissolving pieces
of tissue, smearing.
                  He had fallen
down at the edge of night. Barely awake.
It's all I can do to lift & steady him.
When I hold him still, he fights me away,
flails, hits, punishes.
                    Punishes the one
whose help assures his infirmity. Angrily
looks up into my eyes. "Wait, wait."
I run tepid water into the basin &
rinse out one washcloth after another.

THANKSGIVING

Ironing napkins in the back bedroom
where the cold sun shines in,
I recall slowly the tricks of steam or
wrist that will lay a seam flat
& erase a negligent crease
in fabric that preserves the shadow
of a wine stain, the nimbus of butter
from past gatherings-in of diminishing
family repeating old stories, listing
old alienations until I am left
to host hopefully who will come.
One napkin short of this gold, that green,
to fit absence's place setting.

A LETTER FROM PETER

Waking took a moment, and in that interval
he read so clearly that the burden in the voice
became the scene it sounded. They stood around
in robes of daily life straight out of a child's
book of Bible stories.
                              The edge of morning &
I knew first light rose cold behind the blind.
In their brown and blue robes, all stood listening
to what I heard read out in the letter. A woman
stepped through into what he said, arm out,
maroon sleeve turned back, white palm
turned up & open.
                              What he said fell into
a gap between her hand and him. Not he, no,
not he could place there what she asked.

PISTE

White cross. Red. Later in his life
my father repeatedly told of skiing
the Alps with his German friends.
Of skiing with rented gear, modern
now archaic stuff.
                        Of facing down
the slope in timeless sunglasses
& knitted cap with a golden sun
knitted into it. Of skiing down
for hours, down along a sweeping crest
or sloping edge. Of seeing the red-tiled
roofs of a village hundreds of feet below.

When the cold burst of my own sorrow
swept silence over. Red cross. White.

A KEY

Just before this comedy's over
the lights wheel from cool
to rose. The lost sisters appear
in lawn shifts. A statue
speaks. Brothers shed their
braided jackets for shirtsleeves.
Slowly, one after another, all
embrace.
   Left on stage,
The Clown whispers, "I'm going
to fetch the crypt sound,
for I have the key"
     & runs out
down a ramp through his listeners.

ACKNOWLEDGMENTS

Versions of these poems have appeared in the pages of *Cyphers*, *The Irish Times*, *Poetry Ireland*, *Southword*, *The Summit Avenue Review*, and in *Watching My Hands at Work: A Festschrift for Adrian Frazier*, ed. Eva Bourke, Megan Buckley, Louis de Paor (2013) and in *And the Humming: Poems about Grandparents* (2012); *At the Table: Poems* (2013); *Living Here: Poems about Neighborhoods* (2014), all edited by James Silas Rogers and Tracy Youngblom.

BRIGHTHORSE BOOKS

THE WIDOW'S HOUSE by SHARON CHMIELARZ
"These are lovely poems. I have come to think of 'widowness' as transpersonal almost—it will strike those who are reckless enough to become wives and can recall so intensely the feeling of being in the hospital-vigil with an ending not yet known."—Joyce Carol Oates, author of *A Widow's Story*

SEARCHING FOR MOZART by RICK CHRISTMAN
"Rick Christman's *Searching for Mozart* patrols field, jungle, and occasional tourist trap for the unspoken pardon of art. This quest's 'geography' resides inside as well as outside of the fragmented self, memory as shrapnel and patchy solace. The language here bristles hard-knuckled metaphor as gut punch. Listen, and you will hear his Midwestern credo of disbelief in anything other than the stories we make of ourselves."—Kevin Stein, author of *Wrestling Li Po for the Remote* and *Poetry's Afterlife: Verse in the Digital Age*

LOVE IS A STONE ENDLESSLY IN FLIGHT by DANTE DI STEFANO
"As the title tells us, love motivates the poems of Dante Di Stefano; love drives them to the page in the middle of the night; love will keep you turning the pages."—Martín Espada, author of *Vivas to Those Who Have Failed* and *Zapata's Disciple*

WHERE WE LAND by DARYL FARMER
"Daryl Farmer writes with brutal elegance and loving wonder about the misfits of Alaska, the stony, tree-studded, snowbound, diesel- and whiskey-soaked stage for the excellent stories in *Where We Land*."—Ben Percy, author of *The Dead Lands, Red Moon*, and *The Wilding*

SPELLS FOR VICTORY AND COURAGE by DANA FITZ GALE

"Burrow down in your seat for a great read. Dana Fitz Gale is a masterful storyteller. With poetic prose that doesn't dally and a hunter's eye for the subtle human acts that change lives. *Spells for Victory and Courage* is gritty, and more than a little thrilling. Fitz Gale's stories are compassionate and tough. A collection reminiscent of Annie Proulx's best stories."—Debra Magpie Earling, author of *Perma Red*

THE SKY AFTER RAIN by D. E. LEE

"This book is fire in your hands. One of the finest novels I've read in years. From its quick-cut movement to the hardship of the characters and all those dark places they dwell. It packs tension. Intensity. Glints of inner light. The work moves with such immediacy and build that you can't put it down. You wouldn't want to. Trust me." —Jonathan Starke, editor of *Palooka*

LEAVING MILAN by ELIZABETH ONESS

"*Leaving Milan* is a coming-of-age novel set in the hardscrabble country of small-town Ohio, where young Harper's survival depend on how much grit she can muster. Themes of growing up and small-town communities are explored in this heartwarming and uplifting portrait of an older teen striving for more than what the small town of Milan, Ohio, can offer."—*Foreword Reviews*

A MAN IN TROUBLE by LON OTTO

"A subtly, intimately linked collection of stories. Lon Otto's thought- provoking characters navigate issues of culture, race, masculinity, parenthood, illness and love—the richest and thorniest problems of the self. This is a moving and lovely book." —Julie Schumacher, author of *Dear Committee Members*

To learn more about Brighthorse Books,
visit us on the web at brighthorsebooks.com.
To learn about our yearly book prize,
go to https://brighthorsebooks.submittable.com/submit.

THOMAS DILLON REDSHAW is the author of *Heimaey*
(1974) and *The Floating World* (1979) and fugitive broad-
sides and chapbooks. His poems have appeared in Amer-
ican little magazines and in such Irish publications as
Cyphers, Poetry Ireland, Southword, and *The Irish Times*. He
edited *Well Dreams: Essays on John Montague* (2004) and
served as the editor of *Éire-Ireland* (1974–1996) and *New
Hibernia Review* (1996–2006), both of whose pages featured
contemporary Irish poetry. PHOTOGRAPH BY SEAN O'BRIEN,
GRAIGUENAMANAGH, MARCH 17, 2010.

Mortal was designed and set in type by Judy Gilats
in Saint Paul, Minnesota. The typeface is Tribute,
which was created by Frank Heine (1964–2003) in 2003.

MARCH 2017